# Tucked Beneath Your Breath

## Whispers of Healing, Loss and Becoming

Spencer Vincent Verdecchio

BookLeaf Publishing

India | USA | UK

Made with ❤ on the BookLeaf Publishing Platform
www.bookleafpub.in
www.bookleafpub.com

# Dedication

For the ones who have helped me
see my innermost truth.
For Rania, always.

# Preface

There are some truths too tender to shout—
so we whisper them.
Write them down.
Tucking them beneath our breath,
hoping that somewhere, someone will feel them
and finally exhale too.

This book is a collection of those quiet truths.
It was written in the in-between spaces—
between heartbreak and healing,
loss and rediscovery,
silence and voice.

There were seasons where I didn't know who I was
anymore.
Seasons where everything I thought I could hold
fell away.
And yet, somehow, poetry stayed.
It offered me a place to land when nothing else did.

*Tucked Beneath Your Breath* is not just a book—
it's a living archive of emotion,
of transformation,
of choosing to continue,

even when the map disappears.
It's about finding love in little things,
in strangers, in friends.

If you've ever felt lost in your own skin,
grieved what never got to be,
or searched for light in the softest ways—
this book is for you.

Read it slowly.
Read it when the world is too loud.
Read it when you need to remember
that softness is not weakness,
and surviving quietly
is still surviving.

*— Spencer Vincent*

# Acknowledgements

To every person who has ever made me feel seen, even
in silence—thank you.

To those I've lost, and to the moments that broke me
open:
You are the reason these pages exist.

To my closest friends—thank you for holding space for
me when I couldn't hold it for myself.
Your love has been a steady light through every season
of my becoming.

To the version of me who didn't have the words yet:
This is for you. You were always worthy.

And to every reader who finds their own story between
these lines—
I hope these poems make you feel a little less alone,
and a little more home in your own heart.

# Stay Slow

Let the world rush past
in its bright, restless blur.
You are not late.
You are simply arriving.

Notice the way light settles
on the rim of a glass,
how shadows stretch
before they pass.

Write poems no one will read—
fold them into corners of days,
tucked beneath your breath.

Let the small things—
the slowness,
teach you how to live.

# Storm

I used to stand in front of the mirror
like it owed me an answer.

Who, if anyone, was looking back.

There was a face I knew to be mine,
but it never fit the way a truth should.
More costume than skin, more echo than voice.

I learned to live just outside myself—
watching, mimicking, a stranger in my own bones.
Trying on roles like coats that never quite kept me
warm.

There was no language for it then.
No quiet word to hold the storm.
Just silence, the ache of not knowing
why the world felt wrong whenever it said my name.
Why the mirror didn't mutter a thing after

I screamed
*"WHO ARE YOU?"*

# Mourn

I've found a shape that allows breath.
A name that doesn't cut when spoken aloud.
A stillness— a peace.

Grief still knocks, soft, yet, certain,
like it knows the way in.
Not for who I was—
but for who I never got to be.

The boy never reflected in the mirror,
never heard called to dinner,
never met beneath the high school lights.
I ache for his scraped knees,
his blood-stained jerseys,
his unbothered laughter
rising from a place I didn't know existed.

I mourn the moments
I spent searching instead of simply living.
The years spent naming the ache

instead of running free inside of them.


Some days, I feel like I arrived late
to my own life— but I showed up.
And that matters.
I carry the boy I never got to be
in everything I do now—
not as a shadow, but as a quiet promise:
to live fully, to love bravely,
to never look away from myself again.

# Compass

Vast darkness—
Floating?
Or are we
drowning
in an ocean?
Or drifting
to the deep end?

Either way,
we may be lost.

Please—
Just put your
faith in me.

# Say It

Say what we are-
lovers in turmoil?
Two hearts unraveling,
pulling at threads already worn?
A distant memory still burning at the
edges- fading just the same?

You packed your bags—
Said *"I can't do this anymore"*
Left me shattered,
a scattered ruin on the floor.

What was all of this for?
The nights, the promises,
our home, the ache dressed as love?

You never looked back— not once.
I guess you always knew—
You were reaching for something more.
And I, was just in between.

# Disguised

Fog came rolling in,
too thick to see through.

Lost.
Confused.
Disoriented.

Desperately reaching—
to grasp,
to see
anything at all.

I begged for your hand
to pull me from the haze—
but little did I know,
you couldn't be
my rescue—

You were the fog.

# The Middle

It's not the start that makes us fall,
nor dreams too far to chase—
it's the middle, where the quiet doubt
begins to take up space.

When progress slows to silent steps
and joy begins to fade,
when every win feels far away,
and effort goes unpaid.

But struggle isn't failure's twin,
and doubt is not a sign
that you were wrong,
or running out of time.

The middle is where courage lives,
where growth hides in the strain.
Where those who keep on walking
learn the meaning found in pain.

So if you're lost, don't turn around—
you're closer than you know.
Keep going through the mess of it—
it's where the real ones grow.

# Sunday Morning

Watching the sunrise
listening to birds sing their songs,
sipping a freshly brewed coffee.
Feeling the warmth of the mug.
Feeling a hug from the sun.
Thinking of every moment
that had to happen,
for me to be here-
Right
where
I
am.

# Light Bows

The sunset isn't death, but rest—
a weary sky undressing west.
A quiet flame, a final breath,
not absence, but a softer depth.

It stains the clouds with whispered gold,
a beauty felt, but never told.
It teaches us to dim with grace—
to end, but leave a trace.

And when the hush of night has passed,
the morning finds the dark at last.
The sun returns—not to erase,
but to redeem the shadow's place.

It rises not with boast or sound,
but spills its warmth on broken ground.
A vow without a need to prove—
just light, again, with quiet move.

So let the dusk be what it is—
not loss, but grace the day still gives.
And let the dawn, in hush and hue,
remind you: endings birth the new.

# Best Kind

Some people don't need to try-
they just walk into a room
and suddenly,
life feels more possible.

They breathe,
and your remember to.
They laugh and the world softens.

Just by being,
they remind you
how to be.

And I wonder-
do they know?

The quiet kind of beauty
they carry and how
it changes everything
without a single word.

# Anchored & Free

I want a love that sets my soul on fire—
not with chaos
but with clarity.
The kind of fire that doesn't
destroy but reveals—
softly illuminating
all the hidden rooms within me.

A love that doesn't just lift
but roots me—
deep into myself,
while carrying me above the clouds.
A love that says:
*"You can be both anchored and free.*
*You can fly without forgetting*
*just where you call home."*

I want a gentle love.
Not timid—
but tender, intentional.

The kind that pays attention to quiet things—
the pauses between sentences,
the weight between glances,
the way silence can feel like safety.

I want a soul that meets mine
not with fireworks but warmth—
the steady kind, the kind that lingers
long after the light has gone.

A love that doesn't rush in
shouting promises,
but arrives softly,
and stays.

# Blue Sweater

In a soft blue sweater
calm as the sea.
She walks like a whisper,
drifts right into me.
No diamonds or gold,
no loud display,
just sunlight caught
in a quiet way.

Her laughter hides in the folds of her sleeves,
like secrets the morning forgot to leave.
She speaks and the world,
it learns how to hush,
the trees lean closer,
the skies softly blush.

She doesn't know—
how could she see?
The way her presence
redefines "pretty".

Not bold,
not loud,
not trying to shine.
Beauty simply etched
into every line.

So here I stand,
not saying much,
but every glance feels
like our souls touch.

Maybe she'll never quite know it's true—
how I fell for a girl in a sweater of blue.

# Your Name Here

You calm my soul
the way the sound
of birds on a
Spring morning do.

Awe-inspiring,
A breath of fresh air
deep into my lungs
rejuvenating my whole
entire being.

Did you notice it
in the way I look at you?
That my world stops
whenever I'm near you?

I try to play to cool
but really I don't
know what to do.

Captivated in all
that you are.
I can only pray
that you see
me too.

# Hello?

I almost reached for you today—
a ghost of thoughts I chased away.
Years of laughter, now a blur,
and still, I wondered how you were.

You were the piece I couldn't hold,
a story sweet, then cracked and cold.
You left me scattered, star to dust—
a galaxy of broken trust.

But time's a thief with gentle hands,
it dulls the blade, it loosens strands.
And in the quiet, late and still,
I sometimes feel the aching thrill.

Not love- not quite- but something near,
a pull that flickers through the years.
The kind that makes you close your eyes
and almost send a soft *"hi."*

What would I say? That I still stand,
with steadier voice and softer hands?
That healing came in quiet waves—
not all at once, but through a haze.

Or would I ask if echoes stay
in corners where we used to lay?
Would you reply with grace, or blame—
a distant face that almost wore my name?

I never send it, a mild ache,
a silence only time can break.
Some love was never meant to last,
but taught me how to leave the past.

# Endless Dance

The sun, a sovereign,
cloaked in flame,
who wakes the world
and to call it by name.
He walks with pride
through skies of gold,
a story of heat
and glory told.

He rules the hours with sharp light,
chasing shadows into fight.
Yet even kings must bow in grace—
and so he yields the sky his place.

The moon, a poet dressed in pearl,
undressing the sky with every swirl,
revealing constellations
like forgotten verses.
She doesn't burn— she gently glows,
a keeper of what the twilight knows.

She writes in silver across the tide,
her wisdom soft, her power wide.
While he ignites, she quiets the air-
a whispered hymn, a lovers prayer.

They never meet, yet always chase,
a longing carved in time and space.
He sings in fire, she dreams in tune—
The endless dance of the
Sun and Moon.

# 16. Cosmic Redirection

It's easy to believe
everything is falling apart
when the path crumbles
beneath your feet.
When the call goes unanswered,
the love slips away,
dreams dissolve
before ever fully arriving.

But not all endings are failures.
Not all losses
are punishment.

Sometimes the universe
is simply clearing space—
deliberately,
for what's meant to find you
once you're no longer holding
what was never yours to keep.

It won't always feel kind.
It comes dressed as heartbreak,
wrapped in silence,
wearing the face of everything
you thought would last.

But slowly,
you will look back and see—
it was never falling apart.
It was forming together in
a language
only the stars could read.

# 17. Safety

Give your fears to me—
to burn
to wash away.
Give your hand to me-
I promise, it's okay.

I'll put down my walls
so that you know
you can find safety here—
with me.

I'll hold your traumas
in my hands.
Walk them right
to the sea.
We'll watch them drift
towards the horizon,
getting smaller
while you feel stronger.

For as long as
you'll have me—
I'll be here.
For you.
For us.

# 18. With You

A slow life with you—
Oh, what a thought.

Lazy Sunday mornings,
dressed in only covers and
hints of sunlight.

Sipping coffee on the roof,
enjoying a walk downtown,
hell, even folding laundry.

The kind of life
where days seamlessly
merge with night.
Where foundation
outweighs "expectation."

A slow life with you—
Oh, what a thought.

# 19. Eternal Flame

I gather pieces left behind—
the parts they taught me not to find.
The voice they dimmed, the light they stole,
the name I whispered to stay whole.

At first, I walked with quiet feet,
afraid to own what felt complete.
But healing doesn't beg to stay—
it rises slowly, anyway.

I learned the stars don't owe me proof
to shine within my inner truth.
That love is not a game or lack,
and those who take don't get me back.

Now I walk without their weight,
no need to bend, or hesitate.
I am the spark they tried to claim—
untouched, unburned, and still my flame.

# 20. Home

I was a house with the lights down low,
a shell of warmth I didn't know.
The rooms were filled with borrowed sound,
but none that kept me truly found.

I wore new lives like second skin,
but none would fit the fire within.
Each path I walked, a strangers gate—
too sharp, too quiet, or simple too late.

I didn't break like shattered glass—
I cracked like earth when seasons pass.
The kind of split that begs for rain,
not to destroy, but to explain.

Beneath the dust, a breath remained—
a pulse untouched, a truth unnamed.
And so I knelt with empty hands,
and meet myself where silence stands.

No map was drawn, no sign was near—
just one faint voice I learned to hear.
A whisper not of who I've been,
but teaching me where to begin.

I built a home behind my eyes,
no need for walls or alibis.
And now I walk, not seeking more—
but rooted deeper than before.

No longer lost,
no need to roam—
I wasn't seeking,
I was coming home.

# 21. Waiting

I held out a cup to the breath of the sky,
trusting the hush was a soft reply.
But silence is clever when dressed as grace—
it lingers long in an empty place.

I carved out space in the shape of a flame,
lit it with care, though they never came.
A lighthouse stands for those who roam—
but not all ships are seeking home.

I spoke in signs the heart might send,
soft words that folded at the end.
And though I waited, deeply stirred—
some calls were never meant to be heard.

And though I waited, soul unlearned—
some hearts are meant to go unreturned.

Still, here I stand—unchosen, yes—
but full of love, not made for less.

For even in the unanswered ache,

there's beauty in the risk we take.

34

www.ingramcontent.com/pod-product-compliance
Lightning Source LLC
Chambersburg PA
CBHW071233140726

47996CB00007B/2589